Life Throws Many Curves; Just let God be Your Coach

Ashley B. Maxwell

Copyright © 2006 by Ashley B. Maxwell

Life Throws Many Curves; Just let God be Your Coach
by Ashley B. Maxwell

Printed in the United States of America

ISBN 1-60034-580-8

All rights reserved solely by the author. The author guarantees all contents are original and do not infringe upon the legal rights of any other person or work. No part of this book may be reproduced in any form without the permission of the author. The views expressed in this book are not necessarily those of the publisher.

Unless otherwise indicated, Bible quotations are taken from King James Version. Copyright © 1990 by Thomas Nelson, Inc.

www.xulonpress.com

Contents

Pitch 1: The past is the past; so why hold on?...11
Pitch 2: Life is Life..15
Pitch 3: life throws many curves, just let God be your coach. 21
Pitch 4: Stop kicking, and start picking.............27
Pitch 5: The operating room. 31
Pitch 6: Climbing the mountain:......................35
Pitch 7: Overcoming the world; get in the word..39
Pitch 8: Study and you will pass.......................45
Pitch 9: Take shelter, here comes the storm.......49
Pitch 10: Don't rush; wait....................................53
Pitch 11: It all depends on who you know..........57
Pitch 12: Gods love...61
Pitch 13: Called and equipped. 65
Pitch 14: People say you can't; God says you can. 69
Pitch 15: Praise Him. 73

Pitch 16:	No need to worry.	77
Pitch 17:	Keep walking, it's great exercise.	81
Pitch 18:	A chance.	85
Pitch 19:	Can you hear me; can you hear me now?	89
Pitch 20:	Running late.	93
Pitch 21:	We are all human.	97
Pitch 22:	Keep pushing, the walls will fall down.	101
Pitch 23:	Coming out of the drought.	105
Pitch 24:	Under our feet.	109
Pitch 25:	Removing the hindrance.	113

Introduction

Throughout this book you will read about different pitches that may come your way throughout life. When a pitch comes across the plate what do you do? Do you strike out and give up or do you keep playing the game, and try harder the next time at bat? This book will prepare you on how to deal with each pitch. I realize that some pitches can be a little harder than others, but your coach will teach you how to make contact. It's true, life throws many curves, but who is the coach of your team?

First, I would like to dedicate this book to my brother; Drew. He has encouraged me a lot throughout life. He has taught me not to give up and that someone could always have it worse than you.

Second, to my Mom and Dad for always sticking by me and teaching me that with God all things are possible.

Third, my Granny and Papa for always teaching me to cling to the word of God and everything would come together for the good.

Fourth, to my family and friends (Lynelle, Cathy, Shane and Cindy), for giving me advice and support everyday while writing this book.

Finally, I would like to thank the people who have caused hurt, pain, and disappoint. It was through the obstacles that I had to face that made this book a success.

Pitch 1
The past is the past, so why hold on

> *Mark 11:25 "And whenever you stand praying if you have Anything against anyone, forgive him, that Your father in heaven may also forgive you Your trespasses."*

The past is the past so why do we hold on? So many times it's hard to let the past go. I know because I have been guilty of it myself. We as people hold on to past hurt, disappointments and ones who have talked about us and put us down. If you hear someone has talked bad about you, you are ready to go confront that person in anger. I'm speaking from experience. Instead of making the situation worse by going and telling them off, just go confront them and say, "I thought we were friends". What I am saying to you is they have already made a statement about you and that's in the past, so let it go! God knows the truth and you do as well. I used to get so mad if I heard someone was talking about me. My Granny always said "count to ten", but that didn't help. What helped me was realizing that it's already been said and me confronting them and being mean wasn't going to solve it. The saying "two wrongs don't make a right" makes a lot of sense the older I get. Being nice and not blowing up showed who was in the wrong "the talker".

We can't live in the past and expect to receive blessings. Holding on to the past and holding grudges really doesn't solve anything, it just makes it harder on the person holding on. That's not what God wants us to do, that's the devil taking over our mind and making us hate or talk bad about that person that has caused such disappointments to arise in our life. God is a God of love not hate.

It's very hard once you have a friend you trusted so much that talked about you or critized you behind your back. Or, that wife or husband who betrayed you, that parent that walked out on you, and that boss who fired you when you gave your best and went out of your way to do the job and do it right to just let it go. That's what people think because we are human and it's hard to forgive and forget. In this chapter I will show you how to let go, because there is no need to hold on! Holding on only will hurt you more in the end.

The first step one must take to start to let go is to forgive their self. You can't expect to forgive someone if you haven't forgiven yourself.

The second step is to forgive the person. You can do that by confronting them and saying; "I forgive you and I love you and God loves you". This way you are the better person and you will feel better about yourself. You won't be able to do it alone; you will need Gods help. I know this sounds hard, but with God nothing is that hard.

The third step is letting go. To let go of something, means that you don't hold possession of that object anymore. So therefore once you have let it go you can't hold it anymore. This sounds even harder, but there again God is the healer of all. Once you have let go, you can move on. Holding on to the past, holds you back from the future. Yes, you will make it another day and another year, but you are really not going anywhere. God can't take you to where he wants you if you are carrying excess baggage. Baggage that doesn't belong in your life, you have got to let it go if you want to grow in HIM!

Whenever you go to the airport to fly out somewhere for a week, you probably carry a lot of luggage, (I know I do!) You have to carry the luggage from your car to check your bags in, but you are allowed one carry-on to fit overhead and one that can fit between the seats. By the time you have ventured all the way through the airport to the terminal carrying your bags you are exhausted. You see, you could have left it behind with the other bags, but whatever was in the bag you just couldn't let go! The way we feel by the time we get to the terminal, that's how God feels. He wants to take us to the next level in our life, but we are too weighed down with past issues and that's whats holding us back.

The past is behind you so there is no need to stay there. The only one who holds the key to letting go is you. When I pray, I don't have anything against anyone; I have forgiven all, so my father in heaven has forgiven me and my trespasses. What about you?

Let Go

The past is the past so why hold on;
Holding on to the past keeps God
From taking you to where you belong.

Past hurt and failures, you have to let go;
Holding on will just cause more hurt,
I've been there, that's how I know.

Gods wants us to be able to let go of the past
And leave everything that caused damage behind;
When we continue holding on, that's the devil
Taking over the mind.

The past is over, just focus on what lies ahead;
Don't bring excess baggage with you, let it go
instead.

Pitch 2
Life is Life

Hebrews 12:1 "Wherefore seeing we also are compassed about with so great a cloud of witness, let us lay aside every weight, and the sin which doth so easily beset [us], and let us run with patients the race that is set before us.

This quote came to mind one day while sitting at my desk, "life is life, we have no control over life itself, but we do have control over how we handle each situation we face". If you think about this statement it is very true. We really don't know what may happen tomorrow, we have no control over what tomorrow may bring; but we do have control over how we handle the situation we may have to approach. As Christians people watch us. When a situation comes that we think "we" can't handle, God says "we" can. I am reminded that God won't put more on us than we can handle. People watch our actions, and you never know who might be watching and when they are watching. The way we live our life is a testimony to the world. If you stop and think; we as people might be the only Bible one may read. We can't just be a testimony when things are going great in our life, when the bad comes we have to be a testimony then as well. Sometimes I wonder and question "what if God wouldn't have already been there" where or how would this situation have been? He already knows what we have faced and what we are going to face. Our life was planned out before we existed, although; we as people make our on decisions and sometimes the choices we make, we sometimes have to suffer. That doesn't mean God wasn't there, it means he was there because he is correcting us for the mistakes we have made. What is so amazing to me is that God loves you no matter the mistakes or decisions you have made throughout life.

It is not easy being a Christian, but who said it would be, or better yet, who said it should be? Do you think it was easy for God to send his son to die for our sins so we could have life? That's what people should think about. To the parents, would you send your son or daughter to die for someone so they could live? Jesus had to pay a price for us so therefore; we should have to pay a price for him. That means hurt, disappointments, let downs and failure. That's paying a price, if you don't give up on him. He has never giving up on you! If you stop and think, the more you pay for something the bigger it is and the better it is. Would you prefer a 1991 Honda or a 2007 Porsche? I would choose the Porsche, but it would be more expensive because it's a better car. I shared that so you could grasp the realistic meaning behind having to pay a price to get bigger and better. Usually, if something is free it's not that valuable because you didn't have to work so hard to get it. It won't mean as much to you as what you paid the price for.

So the next time a situation comes and you feel like you can't make it just praise him. Praise him that he trusted you enough to put you through the situation to see how you would handle it. Praise him because he chose you to be that person who could be a witness. Praise him because he will be the only one who can pull you out. He will only put on you what he knows you can handle.

Sometimes we have to go through to get to. What I mean by this statement is, going through tough times gets you to where God wants you to be. An example from my life, I have been hurt so much throughout life by people I have trusted, but I kept pushing on through. I was taught something through this; it showed me not to trust people so much, just trust him. God allowed me to experience hurt, so I could be a witness to the hurting. I actually wanted to take my life when a situation came my way; I wondered why God allowed me to have to go through what I had to go through. I have to say that I was mad at God, but my eyes were open. I can now say, with God on your side you can make it through anything.

No matter the situation, God will bring you out, but you have to want out. You have to also serve him and not the world. What I mean by serving him, is not going to church every time the doors are open, it means having an intiment relationship with him. It's more than just going through the motions; you have to really have it on the inside. A hunger, which I can't put into words.

As I close this chapter, we don't know what tomorrow holds, but we know who holds tomorrow. He has already been there and made your path clear, so no matter the situation it is going to be alright. It will be up to you how you will handle what will come your way; He has already been there.

Life is Life

Life is life; we have no control over what may come
our way; The only thing we have control over is
how we handle Each situation we face,
day after day.

People watch our actions and listen to our words we
say; So be careful to what comes out, when things
don't go your way.

God is right by your side along the way;
We make our on choices, will we stay
Close to him, or will we drift away?

Life Throws Many Curves; Just let God be Your Coach

God tries to make our path easier, sometimes
We allow things of the world to get in the way;
That's when we tell God, "I can handle it, and I
won't Need you today".

Life is life; it is totally up to you which path you
choose; With God you will win, with the
world you will lose.

Pitch 3
Life throws many curves;
just let God be your coach

Eph: 6:11 "Put on the whole armour of God, that ye may be able to stand against the wiles of the devil"

Throughout life we have many curves come our way. When playing ball you have a glove to play the field and a helmet and bat at the plate. With the glove, helmet and bat this equips you to play and play the game right. I played fast-pitch softball from the time I could pick up a bat until my senior year in high school. Every game was a challenge, but with the coaches help it made every game a lot easier.

When a player steps up to the plate, the helmet allows your head to be protected from the oncoming fast pitch; on the other hand the bat is used to put the ball into play. Throughout the game, you have many times at bat. The coach usually is standing at third base directing you as to what to do at the plate. As the coach, you can normally see what's going on and pick up signs from your opponent, also you can talk to the players that have advanced to the bases. You give each player a sign as they approach the plate. Not every time at the plate will you have success. You might have two strikes on you and then here comes the next pitch, it was a curve ball inside, you swing and miss, the umpire yells "strike three, you are out"! That doesn't mean that you are out of the game, it just simply means that you have to try harder next time at the plate. As you step away from the plate with your head held low, the coach comes towards you, he pats you on your back and says to you " there are good and bad pitches, you just have to keep your eye on me for the sign, not only that you have to see the ball make contact with the bat". When you go back to the dugout, your teammates tell you "it's alright man, good try, you'll get it next time".

I would like to share with you one of the curves that someone I care deeply about has had to face, that would be my seventeen year old brother. When I was eight years old my mother had a miracle. I say miracle because that's exactly what he is. He was born at 28 weeks, at 3 days old he had a stroke on the right side of his brain, which affected the left side physically (cerebral palsy) and mentally. The doctors gave him no hope at all, if he lived he would only live eight years. Not only was this a curve for him, it was also a curve for my whole family. I knew with God being the coach everything would be alright. Although, at times the pitches have been a little faster than we were ready for, my brother (Drew) always seems to make perfect contact, a base hit every time. At the age of seven, Drew; faced another rough pitch, his shunt malfunctioned and he was lifeless! At the ER the nurse came out and said "I'm sorry but he isn't breathing", code blue came running through the hall and was working with him. This pitch the devil threw pretty hard and just about proved what man had said when Drew was born right. There again, Drew was looking at the coach for the sign. He had 2 strikes and 3 balls on him. God told him to take the pitch, so Drew stood there and waited for the umpires call, "ball four". Drew pulled out and made it through the pitches to get to the base. He will be eighteen this year. Doctors have the knowledge, but God has the final answer!

Curves come many times in our life, and sometimes we strike out, but when we strike out we don't quit. Striking out doesn't mean the game is over; to me it means the game is just beginning. You just have to focus on the coach for advice and guidance throughout the game. If you don't look to the coach for guidance on what to do at the plate and you listen to teammates and people in the stands watching then you are bound to strike out every time. The coach has been doing a lot of studying for the upcoming game so he knows the right calls to make. It's up to you as the player to listen and be aggressive when you are in the batter's box. I understand that some pitches are a little harder to hit than other pitches, but your coach will work with you, so you can make each time at bat a success. Just don't get angry at some of the pitches and want to quit, keep striving to make contact every time a pitch is thrown to you.

I don't know what kind of pitch you are facing right now, but if you allow God to be your coach and watch the sign he gives you, you will be able to play the game and win. It's up to you if you want God as your coach, I know he has already asked for you to be on His team!

Life throws many curves, let God be your coach

Life throws many curves, so that means things don't always go our way;
You could be at the plate, strike out but get a base hit the next day.

God is the coach, but you stand at the plate;
Keep in mind you are holding the bat, so it's up
To you the decision you will make.

God is the coach, he gives
you signs like; Take, bunt, or hit;
If you strike out, that doesn't mean you quit.

Practice is held everyday of the week
It is two times a day;
Its at practice, the coach goes over
Signs, and shows you how to handle
Each pitch that comes your way.

Your coach is standing on the third base line;
Don't worry, step up to the plate, with God
As your coach you will do fine.

Pitch 4
Stop kicking and start picking

> *Ecc 4:10 "For if they fall, the one will lift up his fellow: but woe to him [that is] alone when he falleth; for [the hath] not another to help him.*

As a child I loved riding horses, I used to ride them every other weekend. One weekend while riding, I was beside someone on another horse; all of the sudden out of nowhere the horse that was beside me kicked me in my foot, I know exactly how it feels to be kicked! It was a very painful feeling and the pain lasted awhile and the kick caused a bruise that took awhile to heal.

Can you remember riding a bike for the first time? You felt secure while riding a tricycle, because you had something to lean on and you wouldn't fall. Then

Life Throws Many Curves; Just let God be Your Coach

the big day came when your parents said, "I think you are ready to ride without the training wheels". On your first try you fall! At that moment your parents come running to pick you up, so therefore; even without the training wheels you still weren't alone; there was someone there to pick you up when you hit ground.

Within the first two paragraphs, I have shared with you realistic examples of kicking and picking. Whenever we see a person fall, instead of kicking him down we need to pick him up! I have witnessed on many occasions when a person has hit rock bottom, because of the things that brought him down, we tend to want to judge and push that person further and further down! In Luke 6:37 it reads "***Judge not, and ye shall not be judged; condemn not, and ye shall not be condemned: forgive, and ye shall be forgiven***". When we kick a person down, it is very painful and causes a bruise. This causes them to be numb to the Christian world! No matter their past we need to be the ones to life them up. Everyone makes mistakes and we learn from the mistakes we make. I'm not saying we do all the work for them; all I'm stating is that we be there for them so they aren't alone.

Going through difficult times alone, may lead someone to depression. One of the most recognized symptoms of depression is a profound feeling of sadness, hopelessness, or emptiness. I stated that to say that's why we need to pick instead of kick! Reaching out to one going through the valley, can bring them happiness, hope and show them that

God can fill the emptiness. Rom 15:13 reads ***"Now the God of hope fill you with all joy and peace In believing, that ye may be abound in hope through the power of the holy spirit".*** No matter what you are going through, God is there. The questions you have like "why me"? God is the only answer to the question you have.

Whenever God sees us fall, what if he said when we made a mistake or a bad decision, "you will never be anything", "you will never amount to anything", "I can't believe you did what you did", and "you are a disappointment"? How would you feel? I know I would feel very unloved, hurt, and bruised. I'm so thankful that God doesn't judge me for the mistakes I have made, he forgives and forgets and picks me up instead of kicking me down. He tells us "you will be something", "it matters not what you did, I'm just glad you overcame it", "and you make me very proud".

The next time you hear of someone going through a difficult obstacle I encourage you to be the one to pick them! If you know of someone who has kicked them try to stop the kicking and start the picking. You never know, they might have just taken the training wheels off and be riding the bike for the first time. No matter if it is their first or second attempt on the bike, just be there, you never know what lies ahead, they may need you, or better yet you may need them. So from now on be a picker and not a kicker!

Don't kick them Pick them

Don't kick them down; you never know what one might be going through; Pick them up, when they come in contact with you.

You might have heard bad things about that person, mistakes they have made, and where they have been; That's when you say, "it's o.k." God don't judge your past, You know it was Him who sent His son to die for our sin.

That's what's wrong with the world today; We have a hard time forgiving and letting Everything be o.k.

We should love all, and quit kicking and do more picking, It will amaze you at what it will do; God didn't make us so we would be like this, He wants us to help each other make it through.

Once someone has made a mistake, it's from mistakes we learn; So why is it so hard to give a second chance, instead we kick them For what they have done.

So, since this has been read I hope now you won't kick; God says now is the time for you to go pick!

Pitch 5
The operating room

Jer 10:19 "Woe is me for my hurt! My wound is grievous: but I said, truly this (is) a grief, and I must bear it."

When someone undergoes surgery it's usually because something just isn't exactly right with your body and normally there is pain. To some of us the pain might have been there awhile, but then on the other hand, to others it could have been an emergency.

About two years ago my mother had skin cancer on her face. It was outpatient surgery (in the doctors office), and I went to be with her that day. The way this worked was, the doctor would cut out the place where the cancer was and then he would look at it through a microscope and if there still happened to be cancer cells he would go deeper and deeper until she was cancer free. It was a process, and though it took many cuts, which meant going deeper and deeper; he managed to get it all. The doctor performing the task was a plastic surgeon, so after having seventeen stitches there isn't a scar.

Do you have a pain? Your pain may be a hurting heart, I understand the pain you feel. When someone goes to the heart doctor after having chest pains, the doctors after running tests may detect a blockage. The only way to repair a blockage is surgery. The procedure will be placing a stint in where the blockage is, allowing the blood to flow freely. Without fixing the problem or putting off going to the doctor off, you could die! You can't expect the pain to get better and the blockage to move on it's on, without help.

God can heal all pain. He is the doctor who can perform heart surgery and remove the blockage so there isn't any pain. If you continue hurting and don't seek Him for help, you can't expect the pain to get any better. You have to go into the operating room and allow the doctor to perform surgery. In the operating room, that's where the pain you feel is taken away and the stint is put in so the blockage is no longer there. After you let God place you on the operating table you will feel better and you won't have a scar. If you keep putting off surgery then you will eventually die. You can't live in pain forever. So, let God do surgery on you today, the operating room is available, just for you!

Hurt

Today I introduce you to a doctor, one you don't
have to fear; He cares about your pain and
he wipes away your tears.

He has many patients, but he can work you in;
You won't have to fill out paper work,
He knows all about you, like where you
Live and where you have been.

He performs surgery different places throughout the
day; When the doctor gets the call for help, he goes
to the Patient right away.

He doesn't want them to have to wait, so he
Tries to get there as fast as he can;
This doctor is God, I hope you weren't
Expecting a woman or a man.

He is the healer of all, the best surgeon around;
So if you are hurt today, give him a call,
You can be found.

Pitch 6
Climbing the mountain

> Ps: 23:4 "Yea, though I walk through the valley of the shadow of death, I will fear no evil: For thou art with me; thy rod thy staff they comfort me."

Could you imagine getting to the top of the mountain, and never having to climb?

To get to the top of the mountain you have to have the proper equipment to get you there. You have to have good treads on the bottom of your shoes so you don't slip and get hurt. You also will need water so you won't dehydrate and get sick. If it's going to be a long hike up the mountain you will need a tent for a place to rest. You might be hiking for days or it might be a short; one day hike, it just depends on the size of the mountain. Whatever, the size of the mountain; your goal is to get out of the valley and get to the top as quick as you can. You have a goal set as to how long your journey will be. Although, there could be a bad storm on the way; the storm will cause your journey to not go as planned, it was unexpected and it will set you back. You will be at the top of the mountain when you have made it through the storm and other unexpected obstacles that formed while on this journey.

The paragraph above can be applied to our life very easily. We all have to go through the valley to get to the top of the mountain. Going through the valley causes one to realize what it is going to take to make it to the top. When you are standing in the valley and look up, you can see the size of the mountain. Some of us will see the size of the mountain and run before even trying to attempt to make the first step up towards the top. Staying in the valley; doesn't get you anywhere, because you have nowhere to go. If you are afraid to climb the mountain, because of situations you may have to face; then you will never make it to where God wants to take you. It's going through the unexpected storms and the unexpected twists and turns that will get you to the top. We don't have to fear the size of the mountain; God is with us! I know when in the valley the mountain looks real steep, but with each step you take towards the top, the smaller it will look. My question to you is; do you have the right equipment to take the hike? Do you have shoes that will keep you from slipping and getting hurt?

Let God be your equipment for this journey. He won't always keep you from every situation you have to face. Sometimes he allows us to have to go through, to see how strong we are. He will make sure that we will make it through, that is as long as we stay with him. Climbing higher makes you stronger. The journey won't be easy, so be prepared to have to climb a little harder at times. Leave your watch at home, because it's on Gods time when you will conquer the mountain.

Headed to the top

The only way to get to the top, one must climb;
You will have to be very patient, it will take time.
Throughout the climb you might face struggles
along the way; Don't be afraid you will overcome,
God will be the instructor
Each and everyday.

With each step you take, you are headed for the top;
Just keep pushing, and pressing on through,
Don't give up and don't stop.

When at the top of the mountain, you will find
peace of mind; Although, you had to go through
struggles, you made it to the top in Gods time.

Pitch 7
Overcoming the world; get in the word

> *Luke 9:25 " for what is a man advantage, if he gain the whole world, and lose himself, or be cast away?"*

In this devotion I will share my testimony of how I had to overcome the world and get in the word.

All my life I had been raised in church, so therefore I came from a good Christian home. Hearing all of the great messages of how God loves me, and how God will supply my every need. I took hold to all of that as a child; then it was a lot easier. As I got a little older and became able to venture out on my own, it became harder and harder to hold on to the messages I heard in the past and a lot easier to hold on to the things of the world.

Throughout high school I gained friends and I was invited to parties, which seemed very cool. A freshman invited by a senior to a party, it made me feel like a "Big Dawg"! I figured nothing was wrong with hanging out with friends and being at a party. Although, when I arrived at the party, there was alcohol and that was even better! A sixteen year old at a party with eighteen year olds drinking alcohol. If you didn't participate you weren't cool!

As years went on one thing lead to another and then I was introduced to drugs. Drugs and alcohol, I thought I was real cool now. Everyone I hung around did it, so why couldn't I try it? I knew I had been taught better than to do things like that, but what was trying it going to hurt? I had to fit in and be one of them! I felt, it was wrong, but it would be alright.

One night I had a visit from God, it was a feeling like my heart was going to jump out of my chest. It happened to be New Years Day 2000. Everyone was having a great time, but that day was like I wasn't even there. When I got home that night, my knees hit the floor and I said "God I'm so sorry", I knew I had to get my life right.

I started speaking at churches and being a witness to others. Life was great, I had built up a testimony and I made a commitment to God that I would never go back. Someone invited me over to their house one night, so I decided to go. I figured that I would be a witness to them and I said to myself "Jesus went into the highways and hedges", so I can too. Little did I know I wasn't strong enough, because a very bad situation came my way and I lost all I had worked hard to gain.

I'm so thankful that God allows you to make mistakes and doesn't judge you for what you have done and where you have been. No matter what the world offers you it's not worth it. God can offer you so much more. This world is only temporary, but God is forever. It took me so many years to build up my testimony and just one second it was history. I thought the world couldn't pull me down, but the devil knows my weakness and he will work in ways you thought he couldn't. I thought I would be able to witness to my friends, but after the situation came and I started living for the world, it lead them to believe that, if that's a Christian than I am. I've had ones come to me and say I thought you were speaking, what happened? To answer that question, I was stupid.

When you are a changed person you can't expect to go back around where you used to be, no matter how long it's been. The saying is true "you are what you hang around". If you aren't one of them right away, you will eventually be right back in the click.

To the teenagers, God is the only true friend; his word has all the answer not the world. You have got to overcome the world and get in the word! You can't do both, it has to be the word or the world. When you get in the word, yes the world will make fun of you and by this time you will see who your true friends are. All you really need to know is that God is your true friend. He is not slack in what he has promised you! He will not talk about you when your life is going great or when you have fallen. He will be there before you ever call, and he won't get mad if it's 3 A.M. and you need him. Am I making any sense to you? What the world has to offer you is nothing compared to what he has to offer you! The world isn't the one who died so we could have life, no the world offers things to make you die. The world didn't come to your rescue when you were beat down, no the world kept beating you down. The world didn't heal you when you were hurt; it kept hurting you so you couldn't heal.

Today I encourage you to overcome the world and get in the word! The world can't answer every question but the word can!

Overcoming the world

The world has nothing to offer you, better than me;
Sunday after Sunday,
you go through the motions, I see.

You come in my house and sit down, just to
gossip and see who is here;
When they give the alter call,
Why do I see you start to shed a tear?

On Monday you go back to your same routine,
Living for the world, and just forget about me;
It really breaks my heart, all that I see.

I have great plans for you,
I must confess;
If you will overcome
The world, I will show you the rest.

I have given the preacher a special message
Just for you, so I will see you Sunday;
Everyone better be prepared,
They will see a new man come Monday.

Pitch 8
Study and you will pass

2 Ti 2:15 "Study to shew thyself approved unto God, a workman that needeth not to be ashamed, rightly divided the word of truth".

Can you remember in school having a final exam? All throughout the year, you were taught what to study and the chapters to read. At the end of every chapter was a test. That determined your grade, and then at the end of the year, you had a big test. This test was called your "final exam". The exam counted a majority of your grade, if you passed you excelled on to the next grade, if you failed you had to retake the course. To pass the tests you usually had to study, if you didn't then you didn't get that well of a grade.

It was through studying and trying to do well that made you excel.

We often have many tests throughout life. God is the teacher and at the end of each chapter, he decides to give us a test. The way we study for the test is by the mistakes we have made and how we handled them. If we didn't handle them so well, then we learned how to do better. With God, we have to pass the test to be able to excel to the next grade in our life. Its through each tests God sees how strong we are and if we are able to take on what the next chapter has in store for us. Sometimes when we fail, we are set back to take the course again. It's through taking it again where we become stronger. Just like in school, if you didn't know the answers on the test, then you weren't ready to go to the next chapter.

God will teach us, by allowing us to go through different test along the way. He already knows where our destiny lies and he knows the proper tests to hand out to us. Although, it's up to us to study. You might say "how do I study"? the way you study is by reading His textbook everyday (Bible), this will prepare you for the next test you will have to face. As long as you study, then you will pass. With the knowledge, of this book you will pass each test. You will not have test that you aren't prepared for. Although, you will have some test that seems harder than others, just like in school. Keep in mind with each test you pass, the higher you go!

So, it's totally up to you if you study or not. God has already handed out the text book, and I can tell you if you study everyday you will pass. If you don't study than you will always fail. It is totally up to you if you want to graduate or not!

Passed the test

There are many tests throughout life,
That you have to go through;
Did you pass or fail, that was up
To you.

You have small tests before the actual
Final comes around;
In the end I hope you will
Still be standing on solid ground.

Each test will get harder when you pass;
God will take you to the next level,
Although; it won't be fast.

It's a process you have to go through;
With each test he is preparing you.

You can't get there and be successful,
Until you have passed each test;
If you try to go on without him,
You will fail and make a mess.

So wait on him, he knows when to give the final,
Don't rush just wait, that will be best;
By waiting on him, you are bound to past
Every test.

Pitch 9
Take shelter, here comes the storm

Isa 4:6 "And there shall be a tabernacle for a shadow in the daytime from the heat, and a place of refuge, and for a covert from the storm and from rain."

As I was watching T.V. the weatherman predicted a very bad storm was about to hit the county and advised us to take shelter immediately. When someone hears the announcement, I don't think you still find them sitting in front of the T.V., I believe you would find one seeking shelter. If you happened to find one still sitting there then they would have a very high chance of being taking out in the storm. The ones who sought shelter they have a very good chance of survival.

Take for example, last year when hurricane Katrina hit New Orleans; you found many seeking shelter and tying to prepare for the mighty storm they were going to face. On the other hand, you found many who stayed behind and those risked a very big chance of not staying alive. Many lost valuable things that can't be replaced, family members for one. This storm left people homeless, hungry, and thirsty. It is amazing how people from all over the U.S. came together and helped the people who remain. Helping rebuild what the storm destroyed, together as a team.

I would like to apply the first two paragraphs to our lives. We face major storms throughout our day to day walk. Usually when a storm comes, we might not seek shelter, because it's hard to realize how to seek shelter, when we apply this to life. God allows us to face storms, and sometimes the devil can brew a storm in from the ocean, like a mighty hurricane. Life can be going so well, but we don't want life too get to easy. If life was easy, and we didn't have to go through the storms; then we couldn't advance and see the sun shine again. It's through the storms we grow. Farmers always say, "If we don't get rain, what we planted will die". When it rains, you can reap a great harvest. It was because of the rain and the storms, which allowed the harvest to be so big. If it were sunny all the time, then you wouldn't grow.

When a storm comes in your life you need to seek shelter. You may be asking where can I find shelter? The safest place to go until the storm passes would be to God's house. He welcomes you always; his house is the best shelter. You won't have to worry about the walls collapsing and the storm taking you out. Also in God's house he will provide you with food, so you won't have to worry about starving.

If you know of someone who has went to seek shelter; although, while they were gone the storm took everything they had, reach out to them. Just like we came together as a team to help the Katrina victims. We also as Christians need to come together as a team to help support and help rebuild the ones who seek shelter and make it through the storm.

Seek shelter; the storm is on the way. Don't die, grow. The cloud might look very dark and scary, but when you seek shelter it will go by quickly and you will feel safe. Storms don't last forever so hold on, you will make it through. I see the sun and a rainbow, it's on the way.

A storm passing through

A storm is on the way, one must seek shelter fast;
The storm won't last forever, this too shall pass.

Sometimes you feel like the storm will never end;
You feel like you have no one, not even that
"true Friend".

God's house is the safest place when a storm comes
our way; You won't have to worry about the walls
collapsing, Or if you will make it another day.

The host of this shelter will provided everything
you need to survive;
He won't let you die in the storm,
He will keep you alive.

So here comes the storm, it's just passing through;
Do you know what shelter you will go to?

Pitch 10
Don't rush; Wait

Ps. 37:34 "Wait on the Lord, and keep his way, and he shall exalt thee to inherit the land: when the wicked are cut off, thou shall see [it]."

The verse above simply states, that we need to be patient and wait on the Lord. I've known many people who have tried to rush God, including myself. If God has promised you something, you will receive it. It might not be when you want it, but you will get it. We need to think about; God created us and sketched out our life, so therefore; he knows when it will be best to give us what he has planned and promised us.

When we rush God that's where we mess up. Trying to do something on your own time, before his time you will fail. We all have dreams and we all have visions, but they aren't going to come true just sitting there. You have to do something for Him, and he'll do something great for you.

About two years ago, I applied for a job and I just knew I would get it. Everyone was praying and so was I. To my disappointment, I didn't get the job. I didn't understand why. God knew I hated the job I was in, and he didn't bless me with a job I would be happy at. Someone contacted me that day and said "did you get the job?" I said, "no, and I don't understand why." The person on the other end of the phone said, "God is keeping you where you are, because somebody is going to need you." I said "I've been at this job for three years and no one has needed me yet." About two months went by and a lady started working in our office. We both shared conversation after conversation, and finally built up a friendship. One day while working, she came to me and shared with me, she didn't know what she was going to do. She had no money to get her two Children Christmas. I shared with her that I tried to help a family every Christmas. After about a month, she came in one day crying and saying they were fixing to take her house. I encouraged her to bring the paper in that she received in the mail; that stated she would lose her house and I would see what I could do. The job I was in at the time, we had something every year called "the Christmas Blessing", this is where money was raised and would go to a family in need and bless them. I took a copy of the letter stating that she would lose he house to the committee and didn't know what the outcome would be, but at least I know I tried. The women had no idea that I had went to the committee. The day we left for Christmas break, I brought in everything that each child had put on the list for Santa. Right before the end of the day, a gentleman from the committee came through the door and gave the lady a sealed envelope. After she read the letter she came to me in tears and said thank you so much for making his Christmas possible. I looked at her with tears in my eyes and I said "don't thank me, thank HIM"! God sent me your way. Her house was caught up for five months and her children had a great Christmas.

So, you never know why God keeps you where you are when he has promised better. Me for example, I didn't get the job because God was sending a woman my way for help. God wasn't finished with me there, I had more work for him to do before I could excel.

Although, I was trying to rush God and apply for another job, he kept that door closed because it wasn't time. If I would've quit my job then I wouldn't have been able to be a blessing to the woman. A lot of times we miss our blessings because we are in such and rush and we can't wait long enough on God to come and unlock the door.

In Ecc 3:1 it states, "To everything there is a season, and a time to every purpose under the heaven". There is a time for everything, so don't rush and miss wait patiently and be blessed!

Don't rush, wait

Don't rush, just wait on him;
Sometimes, you may find the
Light at the end of the tunnel
Looks very dim.

When we try to make things happen
Before the time is right;
We can fail, even though
We tried with all our might.

God isn't slack in what he has promised you;
It takes time to get there, you have to go through
To get to.

I've questioned why, things didn't happen
when I wanted them to;
I've learned, you have to go through
To get to.

It's in his time, he is never late;
So slow down and be patient,
Don't rush, just wait.

Pitch 11
It all depends on who you know

Jer 24:7 "And I will give them an heart to know me, that I am the Lord: and they shall be my people, and I will be their God: for they shall return unto me with their whole heart."

Coming from a small town, everybody knows everybody; it seems. The other day I was having a conversation with someone and they asked, "How did she get the job"? I simply replied back "it's all about who you know in this town as to what you get." I'm not just speaking from this town, it basically goes for anywhere. If you know someone who has authority, then they can pull strings and make certain things happen for you. Take for example, you applied for a job, but you were competing against someone who has applied for the job that was the business owner's close friend. Who do you think will get it? You're exactly right the owner's friend. The reason for that is, because the owner knew that person and wanted their friendship to remain. It's all about who you know in life as to what you can get.

God has authority over all. In Matthew 6:8, you are told that Jesus knows what you have need of before you ask. With God you won't have to worry about him pulling strings. He will give you what you ask for, only if he knows you are ready for it. God want allow you to go into something that you aren't ready for, because it will cause embarrassment, hurt, hate, or low self-esteem. God not for all of that, he wants you to excel in everything you do.

Don't worry about knowing a person who has authority to get you somewhere in life, knowing God you will be supplied with everything you need. It's all within who you know.

Other scriptures:
Hbr 8:11

Who do you know?
It's all within who you know,
That's what people say;
So the question I would like to
Ask you is "who do you know today"?

Do you just know the who
Has authority while on this earth;
Or do you know the one who
Can supply your every need no
Matter your worth?
Do you know the man who died on a tree;
He also caused the blind to see.

Perhaps, you know one who is too consumed
About their self to recognize who you are;
Or maybe that one you had conversation with
One night while at the bar.

You might know someone who can get you
That job you have long desired;
If you're not ready for it, you could receive bad
news, "Your Fired"!

Its all about who you know that gets you
To where you want to be;
So, get to know the one who parted the sea.

Not only that, he placed the stars in the
Sky and called them by name;
I can't think of any other who has authority
That's greater or the same.

It all within who you know;
Knowing HIM, that's the way to go.

Pitch 12
Gods Love

John 3:16 "For God so loved the world, that he gave his only begotten son, that whosoever believeth in him shall not perish, but have everlasting live."

I would like to get personal with you if I may. I have two questions I would like to bring to your attention. The first question, have you ever been hurt in church by the pastor or someone in the congregation? The second question, have you ever been hurt at work by your boss or co-worker? My answer to both is "I have!"

Usually, when someone hurts one in church; whether it is by the Pastor or someone in the congregation, they simply want to find another church or quit going to church all together.

When one has a conflict with someone at their job, what do they do? Do we just quit working all together, because someone hurt our feeling on the job, or do we continue working? We keep working because we have to get paid, and to get a paycheck, someone must work.

With both the paragraphs above being stated, I would like to share with you what came to my mind about three years ago, when I was facing a conflict in my church. It wasn't just my incidence that caused me to realize it, but I've watched others go through hurt and want to take action and quit. God loves us and that's what we are going for anyway! The church is Gods house not mans! If you only go to church to see what someone is wearing, talk about someone, talk to someone, sit with someone, or go because you want to impress someone, then you are going for the wrong reason! If you are going to church to hear the word and be in His presence, then don't let what people say bother you. God knows and sees all.

I'm going to use my Mother as an example; she was at one time personnel director for the company she works for, that description is to hire and fire, she gained a lot of enemies while in this job, but she didn't quit. She didn't quit because people talked about her and put her down; she kept going to work. She had to keep going to work to provide for her family. It was because she didn't walk out when people talked about her; that caused her to advance to the next step up in he job.

Apply the above paragraph to how we can be when it comes to being hurt in church. Just because people talk and make you angry doesn't mean you quit or back down. That's just what the devil wants, he wants the church to split. Like I have said God sees all and knows all, so you want have to leave; they will be taken care of by the owner of the house you attend. It will be by you standing when all comes against you, that you will advance to the next level in your ministry.

Always remember; God sent his son to pay a price for us, I think that's worth more than any pay check-Don't you?

Gods Love

Still going to work, no matter what people say;
God has never said anything about you, so why
When people talk about us in His house, do we
Treat God a certain kind of way.

Gods love is unconditional no matter what we do;
He never makes a remark and he doesn't judge you.

I know God pays us everyday;
Each persons pay is in a different way.

He knows what we need and that's what he will
give; All have been paid the same, in this statement:
He gave us one more day to live.

It's Gods house where we go to get fed;
So don't make it a place of gossip, let it
Be a place of worship instead.

Pitch 13
Called and Equipped

Ep: 4:1 "I therefore, the prisoner of the Lord, beseech you that ye walk worthy of the vocation wherewith ye are called."

As I was reading my Bible, This verse made me start to think about how the Lord wants me to lead a life worthy of my calling and that I have been called by God to do something. It made me start to fill guilty, because I wasn't really trying to do anything for God. I knew he had called me to speak and one night I had a preacher tell me "That God had a tabernacle prepared for me to preach his word in", but I just make up excuses. After hearing what the preacher said, "I said if you think I'm speaking somewhere, you are wrong, and how could I speak to people"? I was thinking to myself how did I become so special? As, I returned back to my seat, I opened up the front of my Bible, and in black ink I had wrote "God wherever you want me to go, and whatever you want me to do; send me". It was as if God was right there and said, you were willing and from the time you accepted me you were called, I had a job picked out for you.

I couldn't help but to ponder on the story of Moses. After Moses, was called by God he seemed to always have some kind of excuse to give God. You can find Moses excuses in (Exodus 3:11-4:13). In verse 4:10, Moses shared with God his speech was too slow to speak to people. God equipped Moses with a speaker; God isn't a God of embarrassment. God sent Moses' brother Aaron, to be the speaker. This way God used Moses' head and heart, just Aaron's voice box.

This should be proof enough; if God calls you he will equip you. No one should have any excuses when it comes to doing a work for the Lord. God provides us with everything we need to get the job done; it's just up to us to accept the job.

Called and Equipped
(From Gods Point)

From the moment you accepted me,
I had a job cut out just for you;
I've already called and equipped you;
It's up to you to follow through.

You might be like Moses and
Tell me please send another;
I did just what he said, because
He didn't want to speak, I called
His brother.

Don't make excuses for the job I have for you;
I molded and made you to be able to do
Exactly what I have called you to do.

Pitch 14
People say you can't; God says you can

Phil 4:13 "I can do all things through Christ which strengthens me".

How do you feel whenever you share your dreams with someone and they say, "that won't happen" or maybe "you can't do that"?

It probably makes you feel like you can't do it and it makes you want to start and doubt yourself, just because of a remark one might have said. A lot of people have given up on their dreams due to negativity by people. Once you have shared what you want to do and get that kind of response, then it makes one not won't to strive for that dream anymore. If it's not successful then the ones who doubted will laugh and say "see I told you". If you are determined then you can do anything, that's what God says!

As I have shared before I loved playing sports throughout my school years. My brother (Drew) decided he wanted to play basketball and baseball too. Do you think for one second I told him due to your disabilities you can't do it? Just about every afternoon I would get out in the yard and teach him the fundamentals of each game. One day while practicing baseball in the yard, he said "I can't do it". My response back was, "yes you can, all things are possible, but it is totally up to you". He kept trying and trying. At this point he was frustrated. I told him to rest a little while and we would try again. Eventually, he succeeded. It was by me pushing him and coaching him that made him know he could!

I want to share with you; no matter what people say or do to try and get your mind off what you want to do or what you have been called to do, just keep pushing. Everyone has dreams and visions; it takes determination and not listening to other people for it to be a success. So when people say you can't, remember God says you can do all things, it is God who gives you the strength.

People say you can't; God says you can

People say you can't, God says yes you can;
Believe the one who gives you strength and
Pay no attention to man.

God has given you strength to make
any dream come true;
It's all up to you what you do.

No matter what people might say,
Don't start to doubt;
You have the strength, God will help
You out.

Pitch 15
Praise Him

Psalms 117:1 "O praise the Lord, all ye nations: Praise Him all ye people."

I have a reason to praise him, how about you? When everything goes wrong I praise him, when everything is going the best it can I praise him!

I used to question why did all of this have to happen to me? Why did you choose me to have to go through this kind of situation? Then I would get all down and out and won't sympathy, I would even throw myself this HUGHE "pity party". After doing all of that, it didn't make my situation any better. It took me realizing everything I had to deal with taught me something in the long run. I learned a lot from my experiences with friends, family and just people in general. Every situation I have ever had to face I don't regret. Yes, at the time; of the situation I thought I was going to lose my mind and I would never overcome the hurt or pain that lied within, but it was through praising him that help me make it through.

Praising Him when things go wrong, that's when you will overcome a lot quicker. You have to realize with every praise, a blessing lies in it. You need to praise Him for that friendship that ended, family member that betrayed you, the person who talked about you, the husband or wife that left you. You might think I'm crazy; I'm not crazy, just experienced! The reason to praise Him is because he allowed it to happen, because He was looking out for you! Praise Him because He stepped in and saved you from the situation being a lot worse than it could've been. Praise Him because you woke up this morning in your right mind, and you have clothes, and a home! Praise Him because you can read this book! Praise Him because he doesn't judge you for where you have been or how you have talked! Just Praise Him because He loves you just the way you are!!

Praise Him
Praise Him because he created you;
Praise Him because he gives you strength
In everything you do.

Praise Him because He woke you up
In your right mind;
Just praise Him, whenever you
Need him, he is easy to find.

Praise Him because he is always there for you;
There is nothing that he won't help you through.

Praise Him because through every situation you see;
Greater is He that is in me!

Pitch 16
No Need to worry

Phl 4:6 "Be careful for nothing; but in everything by prayer and supplication with thanksgiving let your request be made known to God."

Every one of us worry, some of us worry a little more than others; it's natural.

Maybe you have went to the doctor and received a bad report, your bank statement came today and your figures aren't looking so great, or maybe before you left work today your boss asked to meet with you in the morning when you were leaving at five. I don't know what has you worried. I just wanted to share with you, that you can place all your cares on Him.

God states in His word for us not to worry, but I know it's hard not to worry. In the verse above He is saying "don't worry about anything, just pray about everything." Prayer is more than just "now I lay me down to sleep"… it's when you really have a communication with God, just like you do your friends and family. Go ahead and thank Him for healing you, don't ask anymore just start saying thank you. Go ahead and thank Him for the promotion your boss wanted to meet with you about, it's already been done. Thank Him because He saw how low your budget was and someone came your way and blessed you. It was through not worrying, but praying that made everything alright.

When everything is in His hand that's when it all works out for the best. So don't worry anymore, just smile and thank Him for all he has done and going to continue to do.

Don't Worry

No need to worry, God will take care of you;
There will be no situation he will place on you,
You can't make it through.

Place all your cares on Him, everything will
Turn out right;
It's the devil that causes us to worry,
He is the one who keeps you up at night.

You toss and turn thinking about what
Tomorrow might have in store;
God has already been there for us,
So what are you worried for?

He will protect you, and through
Every situation he will bring you out;
All you have to do is believe, have peace,
Don't worry or doubt.

Pitch 17
Keep walking, it's great exercise

2 Cr 5:7 "For we walk by faith, not by sight."

To have faith is to believe in something; to trust that it is so. Some believe everything we are told, and others require proof for everything.

In our life we face many disappointments, and it's hard to grasp why we had to face them. Some questions one may ask are " why did this have to happen to me, or is this ever going to end?" The answers we get in return from Gods people simply is, "God is testing your faith, and walk by faith not by sight." You may perhaps think the way I thought, it's hard to have faith in something you can't see. That's how I used to think, until I suddenly realized that I do see

Him everyday. Look around at the creation He made, it's beautiful.

I would like to share with you a conservation I had not long ago with a friend. She and her husband were going through a difficult situation. The situation they were facing was a divorce due to drugs! Her husband was addicted to drugs and it was causing turmoil to arise in her life like never before. She and I had several conversations before the actual day of court. I shared with her just to have faith and not to give up. I went on to tell Her that too many people were praying and God wouldn't let her fail. The night before court I shared with her that whatever the decision was tomorrow, just know it's not over! Right before the call ended I told her to call me when she knew something. There were two kids involved, keep that in mind.

About five PM I received a call and to my surprise it wasn't what I expected, but I didn't let her know that. She said, "I can't take anymore!" my reply was "everything is going to be fine, trust me." God was testing her faith and I couldn't let her give up. I told her she had to keep walking by faith. I reminded her that God was allowing her to go through the valley, so she could be a witness to others who have been there. I shared with her, don't walk by what you hear, just walk by the promises that God has given you. Needless to say, my friend held on and kept walking by faith, her husband is drug free and a mighty man of God now!

Sometimes it takes God allowing different situations to come, just to see how strong our faith really

is. You will go through many disappointments and hurts, but God can heal everything you go through. Its through situations our faith becomes strong. My advice to you is keep walking, it's great exercise!
Other Verse: Hebrews 11:1

Walk by faith; not by sight

Walk by faith, not by sight;
It's by having faith everything
Will turn out right.

Sometimes it can be hard to believe
In the things you can't see;
Ask yourself this one question;
"who created me?"

when you answer that question,
you can better understand
who can help see you through;
give it all to Him, and have faith,
He knows exactly what to do.

You might think it's taking forever
For your miracle to come;
If you are walking by faith,
Your battle has already been won!

Pitch 18
A chance

John 7:24 "Judge not according to the appearance, but judge righteous judgment."

It amazes me how we are so quick to judge one by their appearance. It's like they aren't good enough to be your friend if they don't own a certain kind of car, or wear a certain clothing line. When you judge one by the outer appearance, it's really hard to get to someone's inner self.

I can't say that I'm guilty of choosing a friend by what they have, but I can say I have judged one right when I've first met them. That was wrong of me though, because I never gave that person a chance.

I've thought many times, what if God looked at me inside and out and said, "I'm sorry, but you have some issues you need to deal with, so I can't get to know you." That would hurt so bad! Instead, even after he knows all about us (even what people don't know) he loves us anyway. He doesn't care where you have been, he was just glad you accepted Him. He doesn't judge you for what you have or don't have. No matter our appearance He loves us unconditionally.

Don't be so quick to judge one, give them a chance.

A Chance
So quick to judge, just by what we see;
What if God didn't know you when you
Were filthy.

To Him it's not about the jobs we
Have or the cars we drive;
He sees what matters most, what's
On the inside.

He is not quick to judge, even
though he knows every detail;
if he did judge and didn't give
us a chance, then we couldn't
make it to heaven that would leave
hell.

We shouldn't judge people by what we
Know or see;
Give all a chance, like God is how we
Need to be.

Pitch 19
Can you hear me;
can you hear me now?

Ps. 17:6 "I have called upon thee, for thou wilt hear me, o God; incline thien ear unto me, [and hear] my speech."

Everywhere you look these days someone is on a cell phone. I really don't know what we did before they existed, do you? We can just pick up the phone no matter where we are and be in contact with the whole world; that's what we think. I would like to share with you how I look at a cell phone. Don't get me wrong they are great to have, but they don't always work. I pay every month to have service on my cell phone, that way it will work. Although, I find myself at time asking the other party "can you hear me, can you hear me now?" If I don't need to contact anyone it works, but when I really need to contact someone it's as though I can't get a signal out. Without proper service when someone tries to contact you it goes straight to your voice mail and when you try to call out it comes up on your screen, call failed.

God has never failed his people, he hears our every prayer. When talking to Him we don't have to worry about if we will have enough signals to be able to contact Him. Talking to God, we have clear reception and the service is free. Also, when we call Him; we don't have to worry about if he will be able to answer our call, due to Him being out of area.

Let's turn the table now. I wonder how many times God has tried to contact us, and we were too far out; it went straight to our voice mail? One more thought for you, how many times has he contacted us, and we heard him; we were just too busy with our life and going down hill. Going down hill caused us to lose service and God had to say, "can you hear me, can you hear me now?" Always know that God has full service and you will never have to ask him if he hears you. His cell phone is available anytime of the day, so go ahead try and give him a call.

Can you hear me now?
Can you hear me, can you hear me now,
When we lose signal that's normally what
One would probably say;
It is amazing when talking to God,
Those are words we never will have to say.

He is always there to answer our call;
Whether we are in the valley or standing tall.

When down in the valley on our cell phone
We lose service right away;
When talking to God we never have
To worry about our service fading away.

He is available to always answer your call;
Call and talk everyday, don't wait and contact
Him only when you fall.

Pitch 20
Running Late

Ps. 73:23 "Nevertheless I [am] continually with thee: thou hast holding my right hand."

This morning I overslept. I was running about five minutes later than normal. Some of us get a little upset if we are late, all of us do when it comes to going to work. As I walked down the stairs I heard the loudest sound. I rushed to look out the window, to my surprise I watched as two sheriff cars and ambulances were flying by my house in the direction I was getting ready to take.

As I ventured down the driveway, Psalms 73:23 came to mind. I started thinking that the Lord is continually with me, I hold his right hand. I kept pondering on the verse and suddenly realized that

God was with me. That bad accident could have been me. It was Him who caused me to be running five minutes late, and because of five minutes that made a big difference.

God's time clock is what really matters. That's the clock we run on. The next time you are running late, don't get angry. Just know that it is God protecting you from something that lies ahead. Sometimes he sets our clocks back so we will over sleep, and sets us to his clock; he has already been ahead of us and he knows what is best. God's clock is perfect timing.

Running Late

Don't get upset when you are running behind;
When you are looking though the house and
There is something you need, but you can't find.

When headed to work you get stuck in traffic
You may be behind someone driving slow;
Don't get upset, there is a reason you can't go.

God is protecting you, he knows what lies ahead of you;
Our clocks really don't matter, it's his clocks we have
Been set to.

So the next time you are running late,
Just remember you are in God's care;
Even if you are thirty minutes late,
At least you made it there.

Pitch 21
We are all human

Romans 3:23 "For all have sinned and come short of the glory."

Throughout life we all make mistakes or crazy decisions. At the time of having to make the decision, we feel as though we have made the right choice. After awhile, God; gradually shows us through signs of people, that the choice we have made is not exactly the best for us. It's totally up to us to take heed to the signs and listen to the people who are sent our way by God to give us advice.

I know at times it's hard to listen to what people tell us, because we think in our minds that we know best. I am speaking from experience. So many times, I've had signs and people come my way, they simply show and tell me what I don't want to hear. I have always said, "I know what I'm doing and I won't allow myself to get hurt." The older I get, the more I realize that; people are on the outside looking at the whole situation and the realize what's coming before I ever do.

That's how God is with us, he knows that lies in front of you and he tries to direct you in the right direction. At times we tell God, "I know what I'm doing, get back." So, he steps aside and lets you make your own mistake. Although; he doesn't stay pushed away. After you realize you have made the wrong decision, he is right back with you; helping you along the way.

That's how we need to be, being there for each other no matter the mistake one might have made. We need to understand that we have all been there, and show them there is a way out. We all need to realize that none are perfect and "all have sinned and fell short of the glory." We are human!

We are all human

We all make choices throughout life,
Some are good and some are bad;
The bad ones we choose, makes God mad.

Although, he forgives us the moment we ask Him too;
The choices we make, we have to suffer,
No matter what He will see us through.

Life Throws Many Curves; Just let God be Your Coach

We are all human; mistakes are what we learn from;
God accepts all who ask, He will save you
When your world appears to come undone.

No matter your past he loves you still;
There is nothing fake about God, He is real!

Pitch 22
Keep pushing; the walls will fall down

Ps 89:40 "Thou hast broken down all the hedges; thou hast brought His strong holds to ruin."

Have you ever been in a conservation with someone that has been hurt, and they tell you that they have walls around their heart? They have put the walls up to guard their heart so they won't be hurt again. I've been there, so I know all about it. My walls were of hurt, anger, and trust. I will share what caused my walls to be built in a moment.

First, I would like to tell you, that me keeping the walls up didn't help me; it hurt me. The reason it didn't help was, because I had people that came into my life that wanted to love me like I needed to be loved. I couldn't let them because of the walls that surrounded my heart. I want you to know that it's through trusting Him and allowing Him to do what needs to be done, the walls will fall. God can give you a new heart and a new spirit (Eze 36:26). When you have allowed God to give you both of the above, then you will forgive and forget the one's who caused the walls to be built.

As an eight year old little girl I had a very bad experience, this experience caused my life to change drastically. I went somewhere with a man that I considered a friend of mine. I trusted this man and felt comfortable around him, I didn't think there would be any reason for me to be scared of him. He was always real nice to me. On the way back home that night, he started fondling me. I was scared to death, didn't know what to do or where to go! His words to me were "if you tell anyone, I will kill you." This caused me to build a wall of trust, anger, and hurt towards men. Every time I would see a man I would be scared. I hated men all together! I dated people and the relationships were weird, simply because I couldn't show affection towards them. I was scared of letting any man get close to me. After ten years had passed by, my mom started to question things; so I told her and my Dad. After sharing it with them I felt a little better. But the walls still stood very strong! My Mom wanted me to go see a psychiatrist (don't get me wrong, they are good to talk too).

One day I went in for a session, I realized it was up to me to let the walls down that stood guard. The walls wouldn't disappear until I push them down. I had to keep pushing until they would fall; that's what I thought. My Granny happened to go with me on this session that day and when I came out we had a long discussion on the way home. My Granny is a mighty woman of God and happens to be my prayer warrior. As we were talking that day, she made a statement and I will never forget it as long as I live. She looked at me and said, "you can continue to pay $100 a hour, that's your business; but until you give your situation to God, then it will always remain." I can honestly say that I have never stepped foot back in that office. I prayed for God to take away the walls that had been built for many years. I thought it was totally up to me, but I knew I would need His help and I knew He could. For years, I blamed myself and it wasn't my fault. I was an innocent eight-year-old little girl; with God's help I saw that I wasn't guilty of anything.

Today, I can speak openly about it and I show a lot more affection than I used too. It took many hours of talking one on one with God before the walls fell completely.

I don't know what kind of walls may be built in your life, but I know God can push the walls down if you allow Him to. I thought I would never be able to talk openly about it or get past it, but the moment I gave it all to God the walls starting falling piece by piece.

Today I encourage you to let God gradually push the walls down that have you bound. You are only hurting yourself more by allowing the walls to remain. Let God do it, but the first step you must take is give it over to Him. Remember this thought, "it's hard for someone to see the real you."

Keep pushing; the walls will fall

There are different type of walls on can have built,
It all depends on what they've went through;
The walls can totally fall; it depends on whom you
talk to.

Going through life with a wall guarding you heart,
It can only hurt one more;
It causes one to hold back a lot,
Just like one trying to walk through
A closed door.

God's the only one who can give you
A new heart and spirit too;
This will cause you to forgive and
Forget when you accept these two.

I have been right where you are
That's how I know how you feel;
You have to take it to God, He is
The only one who can heal.

Pitch 23
Coming out of the drought

Isa 58:11 "and the Lord shall guide thee continually, and satisfy thy soul in the drought, and make fat thy bones: and thou shalt be like a spring of water, whose water fail not."

I can recall about four years ago going through a major drought. We had very little rain that year, and without rain trees started dying, rivers and lakes started drying up, everything just looked so bare. The way it looked, you would've thought there wasn't hope for anything. One day the rain started falling and the trees started growing, rivers and lakes started filling back up and everything looked so beautiful, just like a drought had never taken place.

You can apply a drought to our spiritual life. If you don't get fed properly, then you will eventually go into a drought and die spiritually. For one to be fed properly you must read His word and have a relationship with Him. You can't expect to grow spiritually without the proper amount of food.

One might think, "I don't feel what I used to feel when I'm in His presence." To answer that thought, maybe you have got in a comfort zone, and God is expecting more out of you, before He will do more for you. Another might think, "there is no hope for me." Can I share something with you, in the first paragraph I stated that there wasn't any hope for the trees and rivers and lakes when we were in a drought, but the moment the rain came everything looked beautiful as though there hadn't been a drought. There is hope for you!

So, that lets me know that no matter how far gone one may feel spiritually, God will send the rain back into our life. Hold on my friend, here comes the rain; you are coming out of the drought!

Coming out of the drought

When we are spiritually in a drought;
We seem to think there is no way out.

We seem not to feel the way we used to feel;
Go won't let you die, His love is so real.

Life Throws Many Curves; Just let God be Your Coach

You may think you have gone too far
And there seems to be no hope for you;
Don't let the enemy put thoughts in you mind,
God will continually guide you through.

Maybe right now you are experiencing a drought;
God is sending the rain, just believe and don't
doubt.

Pitch 24
Under our feet

Romans 16:20 "and the God of peace shall bruise Satan under your feet shortly. The grace of God be with you."

I am so fed up with the devil, how about you? It seems as though he is always coming against me and trying to tear me down. Whenever I would face difficulties, I would never put up a fight to the enemy. He always knew the things of the world that would tempt me and I would fail. I would turn right back to the worldly things whenever something would come my way, that's just what the enemy wanted. Finally, one day I decided I have had enough of him and he was no longer going to steal my joy, peace, and love for others.

It always seems like whenever we get in the word, that's when the enemy will throw things up at you from the world. I understand it all now, he knows that the word will give you peace, joy, and teach you not to hate. So, he will try everything in his power to get you back to his world. That's right where he wants you! You might say, "I don't go to church and I'm happy." The devil has you convinced that you are happy, that's his job. A thought for you, "things of this world are only temporary."

God has promised you a lot more than anything the enemy can give, it's something that's forever and not something that's just temporary and will die! I encourage you, the next time the enemy comes knocking at your door, declare that nothing can put joy in your soul like Jesus can! Nothing can give you peace of mind like Jesus! Nothing can make you love your enemies only Jesus can!

Don't let the enemy win, bury him under your feet and cling to Romans 6:20, and know that "the grace of God is with you forever!"

Under our Feet

Feed up with the enemy, I know
How you feel;
I'm so tired of him coming into
My life to steal.

I used to be afraid when he
Would come to attack;
But one day, I got so fed up,
Everything he had stole, I
Took it all back.

I put him under my feet, and
That's where he will stay;
The world had nothing to offer,
A accepted Christ and promised
To go His way.
The devil is defeated and lies under my feet;
Now, I'm a child of God and no longer weak.

Put the enemy under your feet,
you will become strong;
In God's kingdom is where you belong.

Pitch 25
Removing the hindrance

Job 9:12 "Behold he taketh away, who can hinder Him? Who will say unto Him, what doest thou?"

Throughout this past year, a lot of people whom have been a part of my life for many years, ties have been cut. For many months it was as though people were fading out of my life and it was hard to understand. After several months of prayer, and questioning why, it all came together.

One day while I was walking to my car during my lunch break, it all hit me. My questions "why", became answers. It made so much sense to me, although; I can say at the time all was taking place it was like a nightmare that lasted more than just one night. The pain that I felt at times, was unbearable, but I made it through!

The answer God gave me that day, was "He" had to remove the people from my life. I had every opportunity to get out of all the relationships, but I held on thinking it would get better. He said, "I know you weren't strong enough to break them, so I broke them for you. I had to allow something to happen; that would cause you not to want to look back. Where I am getting ready to take you, the one's you had in your life, wouldn't be able to give you the proper support you will be needing, so I removed the one's who would hinder you from your destiny. I had to replace them with the one's who wants what is best for you and I have equipped them to help you and encourage you." This all made perfect sense to me.

Sometimes we try to make relationships work the way we want them to. If God's not the center of it, it's going to be a struggle. He will remove the ones who will hinder you from the calling God has placed on your life. It might not be what you want at the time, but you will thank him for it in the end. He knows where you are headed and he knows what is best for you!

I can tell you this because I have been there and made it through! God will remove the hindrance, although he will replace them with the helping. God knows what lies ahead; he knows who will be able to take all he has in store for you.

Removing the hindrance

He will remove some that you think you can't live without; Those were probably the ones who didn't encourage, And always started to doubt.

> He knows what is best for you;
> He will remove the ones who
> Will hinder what he has
> Called you to do.

God gives us a chance to cut ties on our own; By allowing things to happen, to show that in Your life they really don't belong.

We think we can make it work only if we try; God knows what is best, although we may still Question "why"?

God will remove the ones who will hinder your destiny; They will be replaced with the ones who will support and encourage you, in time you will see.

Printed in the United States
65242LVS00001B/76-123